WHERE DOES IT PARK?

Susan Canizares

Scholastic Inc.
New York • Toronto • London • Auckland • Sydney

Acknowledgments

Literacy Specialist: Linda Cornwell

Learning Center Consultant: Ellen Booth Church

Design: Silver Editions

Photo Research: Silver Editions

Endnotes: Susan Russell

Endnote Illustrations: Hokanson/Cichetti

Photographs: Cover: Richard A. Cooke III/Tony Stone Images; p. 1: Frederica Georgia/Photo Researchers, Inc.; pp. 2 & 3: Tony Freeman/Photo Edit; p. 4: Robert Ginn/Photo Edit; p. 5: Peter Vadnai/The Stock Market; p. 6: Joseph Sohm/The Stock Market; p. 7: Richard A. Cooke III/Tony Stone Images; p. 8: Don Spiro/Tony Stone Images; p. 9: Lionel F. Stevenson/Photo Researchers, Inc.; p. 10: C. G. Maxwell/Photo Researchers, Inc.; p. 11: Steven Saks/Photo Researchers, Inc.; p. 12: David Sailors/The Stock Market.

8   9   10   08   09 08 07 06

Where does a car park?

In a garage.

Where does a bus park?

At a bus yard.

Where does a truck park?

At a truck stop.

Where does a train park?

At a train yard.

Where does a boat park?

In a harbor.

Where does a plane park?

At an airport.

WHERE DOES IT PARK?

People travel in many different kinds of vehicles every day. Cars, buses, and trains help us get from place to place. But these vehicles aren't in use all the time. So what happens when they are not being used? They need a place to park! The parking places shown here are especially designed for different kinds of vehicles.

Garage Garages are built to shelter cars. They are often attached to the houses where the car owners live. A garage protects a car from bad weather like rain and snow. A garage can hold one car, two cars, or even more. At big shopping centers, there are usually giant garages with several levels, where many cars can park at once.

Bus yard School buses take many children to school and home again each day. After every child has been dropped off, the driver takes the school bus to a bus yard. All the buses are kept together, and the drivers come back the next morning to do the job all over again! Buses that go on long trips park at bus stations. These stations are busy places. People go there to buy tickets to ride on the buses. There is a place in the bus station to load and unload suitcases and bags, a place where the buses can be checked by mechanics, and benches for people who are waiting to ride the bus. There is sometimes even a snack bar to buy food while you wait!

Truck stop If you travel on the highway, you might see places with lots of big trucks gathered around. These are called truck stops. A truck stop is where trucks get refueled when they are carrying goods on long trips

across the country. Truck stops often have restaurants so that the drivers can get refueled, too! Some truck stops provide places for the drivers to take a nap so they can continue on their journey feeling refreshed.

Train yard A train yard is a large outdoor area where train cars carrying freight are loaded and unloaded. It is the place where the cars can be unhooked and then hooked up with other cars to form a different train. The train tracks can also be moved so that trains can switch from one track to another or change directions. There is usually a small tower in the middle of the train yard where all this switching is controlled by just one person!

Harbor A harbor is a protected place where the water is calmer than the open sea. Here there are boat docks — wooden structures built over the water. Boats park and tie up at the dock so they won't float away. Then the people who are riding in the boat can get out and walk on the dock to the shore. A marina is a group of these boat docks together in a harbor.

Airport Like bus stations, airports are filled with activity. People must come to the airport when they want to take a trip on an airplane. This is where they buy tickets and get aboard the planes or meet friends or relatives coming to visit. Airports are very big places because they must have long runways for the planes to take off and land. Also found at airports are airplane hangars. These are very big buildings, sort of like airplane garages, where the planes are checked and worked on by the mechanics.